Dreams

"Anything the mind can conceive and believe,
it can achieve."

LANSDOWNE

Dreams

UNLOCK THE SECRETS OF
YOUR SUBCONSCIOUS

Frank Garfield & Rhondda Stewart-Garfield

Illustrated by Penny Lovelock

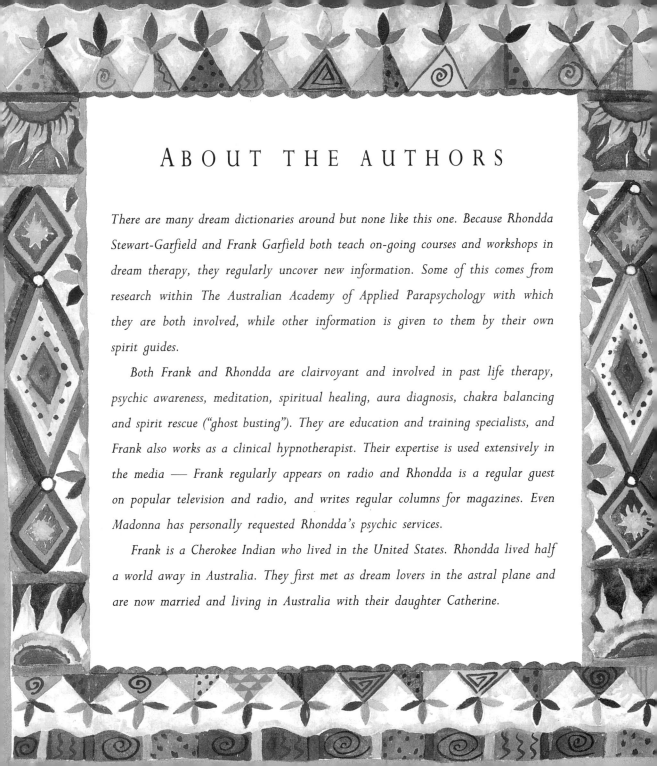

ABOUT THE AUTHORS

There are many dream dictionaries around but none like this one. Because Rhondda Stewart-Garfield and Frank Garfield both teach on-going courses and workshops in dream therapy, they regularly uncover new information. Some of this comes from research within The Australian Academy of Applied Parapsychology with which they are both involved, while other information is given to them by their own spirit guides.

Both Frank and Rhondda are clairvoyant and involved in past life therapy, psychic awareness, meditation, spiritual healing, aura diagnosis, chakra balancing and spirit rescue ("ghost busting"). They are education and training specialists, and Frank also works as a clinical hypnotherapist. Their expertise is used extensively in the media — Frank regularly appears on radio and Rhondda is a regular guest on popular television and radio, and writes regular columns for magazines. Even Madonna has personally requested Rhondda's psychic services.

Frank is a Cherokee Indian who lived in the United States. Rhondda lived half a world away in Australia. They first met as dream lovers in the astral plane and are now married and living in Australia with their daughter Catherine.

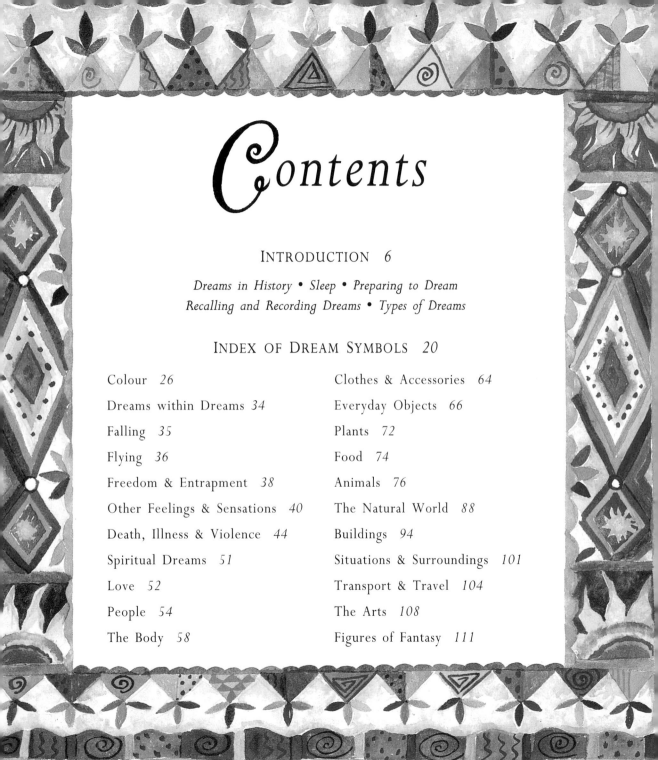

Contents

INTRODUCTION 6

Dreams in History • Sleep • Preparing to Dream
Recalling and Recording Dreams • Types of Dreams

INDEX OF DREAM SYMBOLS 20

Introduction

EVERYONE DREAMS. Dreams are an important part of our lives, almost a third of which are passed in sleep. Dreams may be one of the mind's ways to maintain sanity, to cope with life. We dream about our ambitions, our hopes and fantasies, our expectations, our worries.

From first thing in the morning until last thing at night, the conscious mind registers and responds to the data delivered by our senses of sight, smell, taste, touch and hearing. In the dream state, the subconscious can retrieve and further process this data. By keeping notes about your dreams and reviewing them you should see a pattern emerging that reveals the issues that your subconscious mind perceives as serious.

When you wake refreshed and clearheaded, chances are that during your dream state you have examined an aspect of your life and clarified it.

Feeling confused upon waking might be a signal that the issue is still relevant and you are not sure how to deal with it. The subconscious will then continue to use different dreams to give you the opportunity to resolve the matter.

Sometimes a frightening dream seems so real that you might fear the events actually happening in your waking life. Remember that dreams are symbolic. A frightening dream is only trying to show you that you are fearful of something in your life that you are not confronting or resolving. Your protective subconscious is trying to help you achieve clarity so you can grow.

Even dreams you don't remember are important to this process. Some we don't remember because we are not ready to take conscious responsibility for the issues, or because our subconscious is just processing all the different experiences we have had, getting them ready to resurface in another dream at a later stage.

DREAMS
IN HISTORY

Recognition of the importance of dreams goes back thousands of years. The interpretation of dreams has played a major role in virtually every society that has ever existed. Tribal high priests, medicine men or shamans often used dreams to foretell the fortunes and direct the travels of nomadic tribes. Egyptian papyrus documents dating back to 2000 BC discuss dreams and their interpretations.

The ancient Greeks gave the name oneiromancy to the interpretation of dreams (from the words *oneiros* meaning dream, and *manteia* meaning divination). They believed the dreamer was in contact with the gods. In Homer's *Illiad*, dating from around 800 BC, we can see some examples. In later centuries, Hippocrates, Aristotle and Galen professed that dreams often contained physiological information that heralded future illnesses. Greek healers had taught that coloured, as distinct from black and white dreams, balanced thought with feeling that would enable the body to recover while asleep and equip it to deal with life.

Around 150 AD, Artemidorus documented and interpreted thousands of dream reports in his book *Oneirocritica*. Unlike his predecessors, Artemidorus maintained that symbols in dreams did not have one, universal meaning.

In 1900, Sigmund Freud ushered in the modern age of dream research in his famous text, *The Interpretation of Dreams*. According to Freud, dreams are disguised thoughts from the unconscious mind. He developed an elaborate theory of dreaming and of how the mind works while asleep.

Carl Jung, a onetime student of Freud, further developed dream analysis. Jung observed linkages between those symbols we develop individually and those we share with others. He proposed these similarities indicate the existence of two connected yet distinct layers of the unconscious: the personal and the collective.

The personal unconscious comprises material that has arisen during an individual's life that has been forgotten or repressed. The collective unconscious is an inherited structure common to all humankind and composed of archetypes — innate predispositions to experience universal human situations in distinctly human ways. This essential knowledge of life has been extracted by humans regardless of time, place or culture and stored as examples and symbols to guide us through life stages and events such as childhood, adolescence, the search for a mate, parenthood and confronting death. Highly elaborated derivatives of these archetypes populate all the great mythological and religious systems of the world.

Towards the end of his life, Jung also suggested that the deepest layers of the unconscious, by functioning independently of time, space and causality, generate paranormal phenomena such as clairvoyance and precognition.

SLEEP

There are different levels of sleep, each indicated by brain wave activity:

- Light sleep or the very relaxed state between wakefulness and sleep which is indicated by alpha brain waves.

- Rapid Eye Movement (REM) sleep during which dreaming occurs. Alpha brain waves also indicate this state.

- Deep sleep which is indicated by theta brain waves.

- Deepest sleep indicated by two levels of delta brain waves. Maximum physical restoration occurs at the first level. Astral travel may take place during the second or deepest level.

A typical sleep pattern consists of 90 minute intervals alternating between the various levels of sleep. The average adult experiences five periods of REM sleep which occurs for an average of about 20 minutes or 20 percent of each 90 minute interval. Children up to the age of 12 experience REM sleep between 50 and 80 percent of each interval. There is some evidence that maximum restoration of the psyche takes place during this period. For instance, women have longer REM periods during their pre-menstrual phases to help restore them in this time often marked by irritability, depression, and anxiety.

The percentage of time spent in different levels of sleep changes over the course of the sleep period. More time is spend in alpha level sleep (the period when dreams occur) than in deepest sleep at the end of the period. This is why a person tends to remember the last dream before waking.

PREPARING TO DREAM

There are a number of things you can do in your waking life that will have a positive impact on your dreams. If you can deal with situations, fears and problems in your waking life you will actually release the need to bring out the problem in the dream state. You may do this through active conscious thought, meditation or positive affirmations. Whether you successfully deal with the issue or not, some of the experiences will still be relived during sleep but they will have a far less negative impact.

Meditation can prepare you for a good night's sleep and for the dream state. You might like to try a simple meditation in a quiet place before going to bed — perhaps in a bath full of warm, scented water, the bathroom lit with a single candle.

Many people find listening to music an effective way to induce tranquillity prior to entering the dream state — try instrumental, classical (particularly Baroque) or ambient recordings.

There are many breathing techniques to relax you in preparation for either meditation or sleep. You might like to try this one. Focus inside your mind, and slowly count to four. Inhale deeply through your nose and take the air deep down into your abdomen. Hold it for a moment. Again to a count of four, very slowly exhale through your mouth and as you exhale, feel yourself letting go of all stress and tension. Feel every muscle in your body becoming soft and loose and comfortable. Take a few moments as you relax completely to take a mental tour of your body. Take time to notice anywhere you still feel any tension or stress and let it go. Repeat this process for a minimum of three inhalations and three exhalations. Become aware of how much more you relax mentally and physically with each breath you let go. For maximum benefit, keep repeating these steps for one to three minutes.

RECALLING &
RECORDING DREAMS

To help you to remember dreams, just before sleep, breathe deeply and focus mentally. Say to yourself that you wish to remember clearly any dream that you have. If you keep making this affirmation, you will soon find it easier to remember your dreams.

The contents of a dream can vanish in minutes unless you note them immediately, so if you wake from a dream during the night, record it at once. Don't be tempted to wait until the next morning. As soon as you wake, mentally replay the main points of your dream about three times, adding more detail with each replay. Next, record each dream on a separate piece of paper or with a small tape-recorder kept at your bedside.

Later in the day or at the end of the week you can compare and contrast each of your dreams, seeing what category each fits into. Patterns will become obvious.

When you start a diary of your dreams, it is important to keep a diary of some sort of your waking life, too. If you compare this to your dreams, you should be able to see how the two fit together and find the key to unlocking your personal symbolism. Use your gut-level feelings and the information contained in this book in your analysis. Using this process, you should gain greater insight into yourself, your limitations and concerns.

An alphabetical index of the symbols in your dreams also could be very useful. Without thinking about the dream itself, simply list the symbols or dream images or items. Then list all the ideas and feelings that you associate with them. Remember that there can be more than one meaning to a symbol and, just as our ideas change, personal symbolic meanings can also change. Soon you should be able to determine what *your own* dream symbols mean *to you* as an individual.

Five steps for dream analysis

- Recall and record the dream.
- Define the type of dream, for example, whether it was a nightmare or a dream you often experience.
- Note whether the dream focused on the past, present or future.
- Note how you felt on waking.
- Note the specific symbols belonging to each dream and their associations for you.

TYPES OF DREAMS

Explanatory dreams

These kinds of dreams are about exploring your daily problems. In them, you actually receive all the information you need in order to resolve any life crisis that you are unable to deal with in a wakened state. However, the dream is usually very abstract and you may find it difficult to determine what it is trying to tell you because of the symbolism involved. The dream allows the playing out, through your imagination, of situations in your conscious life.

If there are issues that you continue to ignore consciously, there will ultimately be a subconscious eruption of some magnitude to get your attention. Your dreams may become more explicit, more exaggerated, more bizarre and perhaps even terrifying until you respond positively to the knowledge they offer you. Sometimes a simple conscious acknowledgment of a problem will allow the subconscious to begin work to produce a positive outcome.

Nightmares

A nightmare is a vividly unpleasant, often violent dream that usually awakens the sleeping person. Although some adults have nightmares throughout their lives, nightmares usually stem from an unresolved issue in your waking life and tend to occur during or after periods of exceptional stress. Generally, they are not signs of sleep disorder or indications of physiological or psychological problems such as depression but very occasionally they do require treatment.

By contrast, night terrors — incidents of panicky arousal from non-REM (non-dreaming) sleep — are considered to be sleep disorders. Night terrors occur more frequently in children than in adults, especially in the very young.

Recurrent dreams

The first type of recurrent dream is like replaying a video tape. These exact re-runs might occur once monthly, or once yearly, rather than night after night. The subject is an issue that you haven't resolved and might not have thought about for years until something triggers your subconscious. For example, you might once have lost a key. This might generate a dream about a house without doors or windows (meaning you had no way to get into it) or some other dream which tells you to be more careful about small things. One day, years later, you might acquire a key similar to the one you lost. That night, and other nights too, the original house dream returns because subconsciously you still worry about the consequences of overlooking the small but crucial things in life.

The second type of recurrent dream is a theme dream or serial dream. For instance, you might have a series of dreams about going by bus to an unknown destination. This dream might recur about once a week. This might mean that in your daily life you are bored with your work, desperately want to do something else, but have not formulated any specific goals or cannot afford to improve your education to qualify for another position. So in this dream, you are constantly moving but you are ignorant of your destination. If you were to define your goals and establish a course of action to achieve them, this dream would cease.

Out-of-body dreams

Almost every person at some stage has experienced the feeling during sleep that they have left their body, but not necessarily thought of it as astral projection. The astral plane is sometimes referred to as the fourth dimension, that which bridges time and space. It is an invisible world of spirits and the home of souls waiting to incarnate into physical existence.

Out-of-body dreams are usually exceptionally realistic and vividly coloured. They seldom contain symbols and rarely need interpretation. They occur when an incarnate spirit needs temporary independence of the physical, perhaps for renewal or to access its past and future as well as to observe the present from the astral perspective.

In your wakened state, when you experience the sensation called deja vu, it might be because in the dream state you journeyed astrally and previewed the future which is now evident as the present. When you think about someone you haven't seen for a long time and later meet them unexpectedly, it might be that during an out-of-body experience you met on the astral plane and planned to resume contact in the physical world. In your quest for an ideal partner, your spirit might find a soulmate on the astral plane. This person is sometimes referred to as a dream lover and if the dream recurs frequently, the experience may become real in the physical plane. The out-of-body phenomenon might also explain concurrent dreams, the same dream experienced by different people in different places and time zones.

Past-life dreams

If you have a dream that is expansive, bright, vivid, realistic, yet feels out of context with your present life, seems to belong in a different era, it might be that you are accessing your past, either earlier in this lifetime or in a previous life.

A past-life recall dream might occur when you are attempting to discover and comprehend the meaning of your present life or are about to go through some change in your awareness. It might occur because you have a need to access data from the past to help you in these processes. It also might occur when you enter a career or explore potential talents that you have used in other lifetimes. Such dreams can be triggered when you meet people you have known or visit places you have been in past lives.

These dreams may seem strange in relation to your present life but, because they are played out as real situations and not symbols, you can usually understand what information is being presented.

Index of dream symbols

MANY SYMBOLS HAVE several meanings which might appear to be incompatible with each other and with their personal meaning for you. Correct interpretation involves assessing the symbol within the context of the dream or series of dreams and with reference to your own life. However, it is generally true to say that happiness in your physical, waking state is always represented by something beautiful in your dreams and that fear and anxiety in your life is always represented by an unpleasant image.

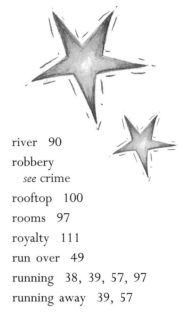

Colour

WHEN YOUR SUBCONSCIOUS brings colour to your dreams, it usually wants your conscious mind to focus clearly on the dream, to remember all of it, not just parts of it.

When you dream in colour, you are often opening up to your total form. You might be starting to know and understand who you are, how you affect other people, what is necessary in life, what gives you great joy and happiness, what creates harmony in your life.

Dreaming in colour does not mean that everything in the dream is in the one colour, but if your dream is dominated by a colour, there may be a significant correlation to the chakra from which it emanates.

Chakras

The major element of the life force within the human body is the electromagnetic energy field (aura) which permeates that body. The body has within it hundreds of energy centres (chakras) that service the various muscles and organs. These are the focal points of acupuncture. However, there are only seven major chakra centres within the body. The chart overleaf shows you their location, colour and function.

All the data that your senses collect during your waking moments is stored through the chakras in the aura. When the chakras are in balance they produce a white aura around the body that indicates the presence of all the colours in the spectrum.

The lack of balance can be reflected in dreams. The dominant colours of a dream about a forest of trees with blue flowers among them, are green and blue. By considering the corresponding chakras, you could determine that issues of the heart, unconditional love and communication are currently foremost in your subconscious.

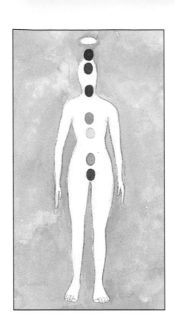

Chakra	Location	Colour	Function
Base	Base of Spine	Red	Expectations, physical energy, physical restrictions
Spleen	Just below the navel	Orange	Trauma, shock, recall
Solar Plexus	Just above the navel	Yellow	Subconscious thoughts
Heart	Centre of chest	Green	Empathy, emotion, unconditional love
Throat	Throat	Blue	Communication
Third Eye	Brow or centre of forehead	Indigo	Higher consciousness, intuition, awareness
Crown	Top centre of head	Violet	Spirituality

Red

Red can represent a deep emotion or blocked problem. It might mean that the body is undergoing healing or that the dreamer is physically very active and energetic. It might relate to sensual experience, sexual fantasies and personal attraction.

Dreaming in red is also a way of releasing, of letting go of feelings in a dream state that you are having difficulty dealing with in your waking state.

Red can be expansive, indicating hope and potential success. The lighter or brighter the red, the more balanced you feel about a situation in your life. If a soft, gentle pink features in a dream, you may be getting excited about something, perhaps a forthcoming promotion or possible growth in your career or a relationship.

The deeper and more prevalent the red in any dream, the stronger the emotion and the more likely it is to be a warning or represent concerns or uncertainties about the subject of the dream. In its darker shades in a dream about employment, for example, red might represent the fact that you are striving for success but perhaps your confidence base is not secure or you are concerned with external influences or other people's opinions of you. The deeper the colour, the deeper those concerns.

If the dream is very abstract or somewhat frightening, your sub-conscious is trying to stop you ignoring the problem.

Orange

This colour represents the level where you store your emotions but, at this point, real understanding about what you are feeling is out of your reach. That type of total clarity occurs at a higher level of colour vibration.

Orange represents stored nervous energy or anxieties. It suggests that traumatic events have affected you. A dream featuring orange could be a signal that these stored feelings may have an effect on your health by creating an imbalance in your system. It could signify the onset of a virus, or that you are exhausted and in need of some form of rest, meditation or exercise to expel nervous energy.

Orange in a dream could also be a warning that an approaching situation may not be as successful as you would like, possibly because your anxieties interfere with your actions. Such a dream gives you the chance to re-evaluate matters and your management of them.

Whether the colour orange means clarity, physical health or success will depend on the specific context of your dream.

Yellow

A gold-yellow dream usually signifies great opportunity and achievement. If the dream focuses on your career, this yellow might represent expansion. It might indicate that you possess great confidence, are making the right choice for yourself at this time, and probably will be very successful.

Bright yellow dreams could be examining the mental activity and different types of experiences that make up your life. This colour indicates you are making progress in either your conscious or subconscious life, and that you are approaching life with the correct emphasis.

Like the sun, shining yellow is a sign that you are in harmony with yourself and your life.

Green

Whatever the shade, green is an emotional colour. A vibrant, lush green in a dream can reinforce that you are in love with life and your place in it, and in emotional balance with other people. It may also amplify your good health and physical vitality.

In deeper tones, green can signify jealousy or uncertainty concerning others. It is a confronting colour that seeks to enhance your ability to understand both your own and others' perspectives and to strike balanced decisions.

Blue

This is the colour of communication, representing clarity and the ability to express oneself well in any situation. In a dream, it suggests that you are either about to or should express your emotions. This is an excellent colour to be dreaming when you are in a position that necessitates a great deal of communication.

Blue also signifies alignment within yourself and a restoration of focus.

Indigo

Indigo is the colour of thought and reflection. An indigo dream indicates that you are or should be practising self-analysis. This is a searching colour that might indicate restlessness with life. It could represent a spiritual quest, a search for more challenges or new directions, or a need to re-evaluate your goals.

Violet

Having passed through the stages of reflection marked by indigo, violet brings you into advanced awareness. Dreams in this colour may reflect your understanding of what changes you want to incorporate in your life and how to activate them. Although they indicate great clarity in all issues of life, both violet and lavender are very spiritual colours and dreams in which they dominate should encourage you to look at the spiritual aspects of your life.

$\mathcal{D}$reams within dreams

WHEN YOU DREAM that you are dreaming you can control events, perhaps even replaying the same dream scenario repeatedly but changing the ending to achieve the best outcome, your subconscious is helping you to understand that you can control situations in your waking life and you have choices available if you choose to make them.

Such dreams are common when you are impatiently waiting for something to happen which you know must eventually occur. This might be a way in which the subconscious allows you to preview the outcome you are anticipating while working through various possibilities.

Dreaming about having a dream might also indicate a fear of forgetting something important.

$\mathcal{F}$alling

TO EXPERIENCE FALLING in a dream suggests that you do not feel in control or that you need to extract yourself from some situation. Such dreams commonly occur when you are unable to determine the cause of your uncertainty or are postponing choices or decisions.

They also might occur when you go to sleep but worry that you won't wake when you should or are anxious about being late.

It is common to dream of falling when you need to wake up and go to the bathroom.

Flying

THE SENSATION OF FLYING, either in an aircraft or like a bird, is widely understood to represent the freedom to advance without any limitation or of the need to escape, perhaps for rest and recreation, to gain a different perspective or to reassess one's life.

Flying indicates that you are no longer stationary and are working towards changes in your life. Already, at a subconscious level, there is anticipation and excitement, and the celebration of new-found freedom.

Such a dream might occur when you have achieved a goal you have set for yourself, or met someone else's expectations.

Flying may represent a change of address or job, or settling into a quieter lifestyle.

The sensation of flying might also indicate that you are having an out-of-body experience.

$\mathcal{F}$reedom & entrapment

IMAGES OF FREEDOM, seeing yourself in the great outdoors or in a vast area in a dream, usually indicate your ability to make choices, to be wherever you choose to be, and that a universe of opportunity and achievement awaits you. Flying is one of the strongest expressions of freedom (see page 36).

If you dream of **running and feeling exhilarated, free and happy,** it suggests that you have finally released a great strain in your life or that you have reached a level of accomplishment beyond your expectations.

Symbols of **entrapment**, such as imprisonment, commonly occur when you feel constrained by necessity in your life, like keeping a job just to pay the bills.

Dreams about various forms of entrapment are common to new parents who have growing family responsibilities and are uncertain as to the limitations this will place on them.

Children resisting boundaries set by their parents might experience dreams of entrapment.

Screaming in a dream is often an indication that you are unable to release frustration.

To dream of **prison** might mean that you are feeling restricted by differences in attitude between you and others.

Dreams of **running away** imply avoidance, confusion and an inability to deal with a situation. Dreaming of **running yet not making ground** suggests that you are stuck in a situation and feeling helpless. Or perhaps you need to take life at a slower pace but are finding it difficult to do so. It might also mean that your impatient self is finding it difficult to learn patience.

A dream of **someone chasing you** might reflect a fear of a lie you have told or some other untruth catching up with you.

$\mathcal{O}$ther feelings & sensations

FEELINGS OF **abundance** in a dream usually signal a growth in your creativity, your insights and the rewards flowing from them which you feel free to accept and enjoy.

Feeling **lucky** in a dream is usually symbolic of new projects, events or people with which you will enjoy being involved.

Feeling **victorious** is often a subconscious stimulation of your conscious efforts to achieve a goal.

Feeling **virtuous** in a dream can be a sign that you have lived up to your own expectations or standards in your waking life.

If the dream involves feeling **trust** in something or someone, it suggests you know that the subject of your dream is a reality in your wakened state.

Feeling **distressed, upset, lonely or betrayed** in a dream signifies that you are lacking in self-confidence at the moment.

A feeling of **exposure** often indicates hurt feelings that you've not revealed to others who distressed you.

Feeling **embarrassed** in public is a similar indication of vulnerability, but also often indicates guilt about some wrongdoing of yours which is about to be revealed.

Feeling **accused** usually indicates that you feel that you are being judged unfairly. If people are pointing fingers in your dream you might be feeling imposed upon or it may be that a situation has finally been resolved.

Feelings of **suspicion** or the discovery of falsehood might be the subconscious stirring your conscious mind to look for deception in your waking life.

Feeling **imposed upon** suggests that you are not standing up for yourself in your everyday life and may be being taken for granted or taken advantage of.

A feeling of **sacrifice** might also indicate bitterness, resentment or anger roused by lack of fulfilment or by your belief that you must deny yourself to ensure another's prosperity or happiness.

Fear of any kind in a dream is widely understood as a subconscious response to the unknown or unfamiliar in daily life or to your uncertainty about the future. Once the source of the fear is known, the emotion goes away.

If, on the other hand, you dream you possess **enhanced or super-human abilities**, it is possibly a subconscious release of frustration at a lack of ability or physical strength to accomplish some task or feat in an awakened state.

If you experience the sensation of **invisibility** in a dream, perhaps you are not letting yourself see things as they really are in your wakened state. Or you may be playing out a desire to spy on somebody to discover their hidden motives.

A dream that the bed is **shaking** may reflect a fear that you will not wake at the correct time and your subconscious is attempting to stimulate you out of sleep. Such sensations may also indicate a return to the body after astral-travel.

Awareness of an unpleasant **odour** in a dream usually suggests dental problems but occasionally signifies illness. Pleasant odours usually repre sent a reward for accomplishment.

The presence of sharp, distracting **sounds** in a dream typically represents conflict and confusion in your conscious life. Laughter, if its friendly or joyous, usually signifies excitement or harmony. Outbursts of harsh or raucous laughter might indicate that someone is mocking you in your waking life.

$\mathcal{D}$eath, illness & violence

LIKE THE DEATH CARD in a Tarot deck, death in a dream does not represent the actual death of a person. Instead, it represents the ending of the old and the beginning of the new. It can be a sign of release and the acceptance of change, especially within oneself or another person.

A dream of death could suggest the elimination of fears and phobias or herald a new ability to take the initiative, perhaps in the form of an overdue confrontation with someone.

Such a dream might mean that you are coming to terms with childhood experiences. Or it might indicate that you are outgrowing childish or idealistic attitudes.

Death often occupies our dreams when we are emerging from depression or despair, and are contemplating the future.

If you dream of the death of someone you know, it is likely that you are subconsciously reflecting the clearing of worries about this person or your awareness of change in a person who has had an impact on you.

It is quite common for parents of growing children to dream of their children's death. Such dreams usually occur when the parent has reservations about the change in the relationship with their child as the young emerge from childhood to adulthood.

If the dead person in your dream comes back to life you may be reassured that something in your life is still the same.

Seeing yourself **walking through a graveyard** in a dream might mean that you are reminiscing about a dead loved one or that you are feeling lonely and isolated.

Seeing yourself buried is often a sign that you are feeling the pressure of whatever is happening in your life.

Pain, injury and illness

Pain in a dream is a typical symbol of a need to release deep-seated emotions in a situation where you fear being judged by others.

Specifically, dreaming of **pain in the head** is often a symbolic expression of stimulus and creativity.

A dream of **injury to the lower part of your body** generally represents self-harm; to the **upper part**, harm inflicted upon you by others.

A dreamed experience of injury or bruising to the **stomach** usually signifies that you have been hurt by someone you care about.

An **eye** injury suggests you are not facing facts.

Dreams of **a broken arm or leg** often reflect a fear of failure, of an inability to complete the tasks set by others or to match their expectations. It can also signify feelings of helplessness.

A dream of **cut or bleeding hands** might be symptomatic of feeling worn out, drained of energy.

Burnt fingers indicate a fear of mistakes, of incompetence, or of starting a task ill-prepared.

If a hand is **missing fingers**, the dream could be expressing guilt and fear of retribution.

A dream in which you suffer **grazed knees** usually indicates that you are suffering from hurt feelings and want a little extra tender, loving care. It also often reflects your need to give more support to your inner child, especially when your vulnerability is being exposed.

Blood featuring in a dream could be a warning that you are doing too much and not only exhausting yourself but also not being able to focus on one thing properly. Extreme bleeding, however, can be a sign of change and that your inner self is flourishing.

A dream image of your body enduring **fever or other symptoms of disease** usually relates to self-punishment. Perhaps you know something about yourself that distresses you, or you have been offended by someone else. Such a dream might also be warning you to pay more attention to your health.

A dream of a **heart attack** might be a subconscious warning that you should take better care of your body because it is being adversely affected by stress.

To dream about a **doctor or a healer** might reflect a desire to be looked after or healed in some way. It may be a message that you or someone you know needs to consult a physician.

Violence and crime

A dream in which you are **being murdered** suggests that someone is suffocating your ideas and you feel unable to express yourself properly. There may also be some kind of threat arising, or you could feel an intangible fear developing.

Being stabbed in a dream indicates that you are upset and uncertain.

Being shot suggests that your feelings have been hurt. You have taken something someone has said or done to heart.

Being run over may indicate that other people are getting involved in activities in which you feel unable to participate.

An accident which involves you dropping or breaking an object may be a sign that an argument is about to occur in your waking life and you will be the one to start it.

Dreams of accidents between people and moving vehicles generally refer to fears that a present involvement (perhaps a personal relationship) will entail damaging conflict or will not meet your expectations. It might also indicate feelings that others are enjoying life in ways closed to you.

If you are the person **acting violently** in a dream, it is possible that you are feeling threatened and are attempting to "eliminate" your competition in the dream state. Your subconscious is allowing you to safely release your frustration and anger so that you are less likely to vent these emotions in the wakened state.

War dreams might also serve the purpose of releasing angry emotions through the destruction in your dream of an arch rival. These dreams are frequently subconscious re-enactments of your personal battles throughout life. War wounds in dreams suggest that you have found it difficult to let go of the past — with each argument, you remember the one before.

Dreaming of the military aspects of war is symbolic of the battles fought in everyday life and business.

An army marching in a dream usually signifies that you are defending yourself with increasing strength, physically or verbally.

Suits of armour are dream symbols of your need for greater protection, particularly during an emotional crisis.

A dream featuring **police**, however, might relate to money, inheritance or legal matters. It might signify a fear of the consequences of your actions.

A dream about a **robbery** might represent the threat of something of value being taken away.

Spiritual dreams

THE IMAGE OF A **spiritual or religious figure** in a dream might signify concern about your death or that of someone close to you.

It might also signify your need to come to terms with sorrow.

A dream image of an **angel** suggests that your spiritual guide is attempting to communicate with you.

Heaven is widely accepted as a dream symbol for justice and also for success.

An image of **Hell** often indicates that you have done something wrong for which you believe you deserve punishment, self-inflicted or otherwise. An image of flames being extinguished might express your belief that you don't deserve punishment.

Love

AS WATER IS the most powerful of the elements, unconditional love is the most powerful of all emotions. Love in a dream suggests harmony and pleasure in life. It is the dream of someone who is contented with their present life and enthusiastic about the future.

A dream of love might also be the prelude to creativity and inspiration or great personal satisfaction through the successful completion of a major task.

Depending on your personal circumstances, it might mean the beginning of a new relationship with that dream lover you've been searching for.

If you dream of **lovers**, it's likely that you want to attract someone into your life or someone is trying to attract you into their life. It might even mean you are meeting someone on the astral plane, someone who would like to come into your life during an out-of-body experience.

A dream of a very emotional **kiss** suggests that you are, or need to be, embraced and nurtured. A dream kiss of the merest kind could reveal that you are ignoring, or even dismissing, something you feel is of little consequence in your daily life.

Sexual dreams usually occur if you are unhappy because of a lack of sexual activity or at the quality of sexual activity in your life. Such dreams might enable

you to release the tensions and experience some of the pleasure not available to you in your conscious life.

If you dream of **marriage** to someone you don't know, it is likely that you fear commitment or even getting involved. If you dream that you are marrying someone whom you know but they appear different in the dream, it could be that you fear the consequences of this relationship. A dream marriage involving someone you love and adore is a sign that you are ready to achieve growth and success. If it is a friend's wedding, it could reveal that you have expectations for someone in your daily life. And if you dream that someone else is marrying the person you desire, it could mean that you are holding on to old loves.

eople

DREAMING OF SCENARIOS that involve **relatives** is usually synonymous with learning interpersonal communication skills.

Dreaming of individual family members usually means that you are resolving an issue with them during the dream state that you have failed to resolve in your wakened state.

Seeing a **sibling** walk through fire or against a background of fire might reflect your awareness of your brother's or sister's personal growth and strength of mind, your pride in them, and the security you feel in the relationship.

In any dream scenario, images of your **parents** generally embody your feelings for them at that time. It is not uncommon to see parents fighting each other in a dream. This usually reflects your worry that they are in conflict in reality.

Unpleasant dreams about your **in-laws** might reflect anxieties about incompatibility and lack of acceptance. If the dream is full of love and acceptance, then you are feeling very comfortable with them.

Seeing **dead relatives** in dreams often relates to past-life recall or to your reliving an experience of theirs.

A dream about an **ex-partner** might indicate that there are still unresolved issues between you or you feel that there is something you have not discussed. Alternatively, the dream might be a final farewell in which you are acknowledging the end of the relationship.

Groups of people in a dream might represent fear that you are, or your property is, being taken for granted or used and abused.

A disturbing dream of **neighbours** might suggest festering problems with those who live nearby. A pleasant one might indicate neighbourhood harmony born of mutual acceptance.

Hearing **people gossiping** about somebody else in a dream is likely to be a sign of your fear that people are secretly talking about you.

The dream image of **a watcher** at a distance might represent your feeling that someone is actually observing you in your waking state and monitoring your actions or performance.

An unknown person standing near you in a dream usually represents someone you would like to know.

An unknown person talking to you represents the beginning of a new friendship.

When you dream that you and an unknown person are getting to know someone new to you both, you might be uncertain about how a new relationship will develop.

An unknown person yelling at you typically represents someone you are having problems getting to know and understand.

When you dream you are in conflict with an unknown person, you might be subconsciously attempting to convince yourself that you will not like someone who has just come into your life.

If you imagine that **a famous person** knows you in a dream, it might indicate a subconscious desire for more recognition for your efforts. If you dream you actually are a famous person, you might be imposing limitations on yourself in your waking life that are preventing you from fulfilling your potential and you should trust in your abilities.

Birth, babies and children

A dream of **pregnancy** represents a belief in growth or inner fears being unravelled.

A dream of **birth**, the coming into being of any life form, frequently indicates your emerging awareness and understanding of yourself and others, self-acceptance, the beginning of something new in your life or the development of an idea.

To dream of the birth of a child, even if it is a traumatic experience, might represent the nurturing of growth within yourself, and being in control of your own vulnerability and strength.

It might also indicate that major, positive changes are imminent for you or someone close to you.

People preparing to wed often dream of a birth as a symbol of a new beginning, and an indication of their excitement and acceptance of the changes marriage will bring to their lives.

To dream of **abortion** suggests either a subconscious purging of some deep emotion, a seriously mistaken view or absolute denial of a person or matter of great significance to you.

To a female, a dream of small and well-behaved **children** might signify her knowledge of solutions to her current problems.

To a male, such a dream usually signifies matters of responsibility or issues involving children in his life.

Difficulties with children in a dream usually represent your difficulties with the children in your life or with your inner child.

Children running away from you in your dream, might reflect your feelings of inadequacy or uncertainty in some situations.

A dream of children running towards you often indicates that you feel accepted for yourself or that you could be successful in resolving a disagreement between others.

The body

YOUR BODY STORES your feelings. If you are stressed, it may manifest in physical aches and pains or the body may become the main feature of a dream. It might be that in your wakened state you discount the importance of your emotions. To protect you from this error of judgment, your subconscious might use images of the body to reflect your emotional state.

If your body feels **heavy** in a dream, you might be feeling overburdened in some or all parts of your life.

Experiencing your **body shape** in a dream as quite different to its shape in reality, is interpreted in many ways.

A woman whose breasts seem larger in her dream than in reality might be experiencing a desire to breast-feed or feeling physical tenderness towards others.

A man whose genitals seem smaller in his dreams than in reality might be feeling vulnerable.

Seeing your own body as one of the **opposite gender** might mean that you are tuning in to that side of your nature in your quest for emotional balance.

A strong, dominant male might be reminded of the gentle side of his nature in a dream where his body becomes female. A soft, gentle woman might see herself as a man in a dream to remind her of her strength.

The various parts of the body have their own significance, as do injuries to these areas (see page 46).

Abdomen

A dream in which you see a female figure with a very rounded belly is typically a sign of prosperity or financial gain.

Images of strange markings on the stomach might relate to your attempts to release anger or frustration and indicate that perhaps your emotions are temporarily overwhelming you.

Brain

Dreaming of an exposed brain might represent deep thought, confusion or uncertainty, or it may represent finally understanding an issue or completing a task.

Ears

Dreaming of ears is usually symbolic of not listening or understanding.

Eyes

A dream of eyes that are bright, alert, or otherwise attractive usually means that you are communicating well with others.

Seeing glazed eyes might be a sign that someone doesn't understand what you are trying to convey.

Face

The image of a face in a dream generally represents an expectation and your uncertainty about it.

A dirty face usually signifies a situation not working out as well as you anticipated.

Chocolate on the face might indicate a better than expected resolution to a worrying situation.

A smiling face indicates the dawn of understanding and harmony.

Feet

A dream focused on feet indicates that you need to deal with any apprehension and uncertainty you feel about moving forward in your waking life.

Hair

A dream of a slick hairstyle suggests direction and purpose.

Ruffled hair, perhaps roughly cut, indicates lack of direction and uncertainty of purpose at this time.

Long, flowing locks usually signify high self-esteem, whereas ill-kept hair illustrates low self-esteem.

A dream that you are losing your hair might be symbolic of feelings of helplessness or an inability to resolve mounting difficulties in your life.

If you dream that you are brushing your hair, you might be starting to take more notice of the way you present yourself to the world, how others see you and how you see yourself. It also indicates that you value others' opinions of you.

If you dream of other people brushing their own hair, you probably approve of them and feel comfortable with them.

Hands

A dream of a hand in the dark usually signifies inner frustration and confusion.

Open hands often mean that something is being revealed to you in its true form and that you are now seeing clearly.

Closed hands suggest that the truth of a situation is hidden from you and that you need to be more assertive to gain access to the truth.

A dream of clapping hands indicates inner joy and excitement.

Handcuffed hands might mean you are feeling curtailed by your own attitude or frame of mind or by someone else's beliefs and expectations.

Clean hands indicate that you have completed or are yet to start an unpleasant task.

Dirty hands suggest that you feel compelled to do something that you don't want to do, perhaps because of peer pressure.

If you dream that you cannot see your hands, you might be worried that you cannot keep up with the demands of your busy life.

A dream that you have short fingernails suggests that you may have to make changes that you are not necessarily happy about.

If you have short fingernails and dream that you have long fingernails, there may be changes in the near future.

A dream of fingers wearing rings, a symbol of opulence, might be an omen of good fortune, possibly a windfall.

Nose

To dream of a very large and broad nose suggests that you are directing yourself towards gain and attainment.

A small nose is a dream symbol indicating a change for the better in relation to your prosperity.

A runny nose suggests knowledge which, if kept secret, will promote success.

Penis

If a woman dreams of a penis, she might be feeling sexually frustrated or sexually attracted to a man.

If a woman dreams she has a penis, she might be unable to express herself as she would wish or frustrated by her own limitations.

If a man dreams of a penis, his dream might relate to feelings of either superiority or inferiority.

If a man dreams of being afraid that someone will see his penis, it is possible that he is afraid of being vulnerable.

Teeth

When you have a dream in which your teeth fall out, it might be a sign that worries are passing.

When you dream that you are developing teeth, you might be on the brink of greater self-knowledge and wisdom or approaching a spiritual path to inner peace.

Clothes & accessories

WHEN YOU SEE yourself **without clothes** in a dream, your sub-conscious is probably reflecting your fear of being vulnerable.

If you see yourself in very unattractive **underwear,** then you probably feel unhappy with your body image. If you are wearing very sexy and attractive underwear in your dream, you probably feel sexy and attractive and find that life is wonderful at present.

When you see yourself wearing lots of **warm clothing,** it might be that you are ill or would like some time on your own.

Bright or patterned clothes in a dream suggest that you want to be noticed or heeded by others. If you are dressed in **coloured night-wear,** you are probably in a state of inner peace and harmony.

Wearing **dark or reflective clothing** in a dream suggests that in your waking state you attempt to conceal your true self from others.

Stained clothes in a dream usually represent something you can't eliminate from your life.

Laddered stockings or **socks with holes** often herald an invasion of your personal space.

Odd socks might be a reminder that you can't please everyone.

An adult man wearing **short pants** in a dream indicates a fear of exposure or feelings of vulnerability.

A dream in which you are wearing clothes that are **too small** for you indicates the presence in your life of something, perhaps an attitude, an object or structure, that you feel you have outgrown.

A dream in which you wear clothes that are **too large** for you might mean you are struggling with a new idea, with promotion or study, or to grow into a new space.

The image of a **hat** in a dream might occur just before you apply for a salary rise or just after you win a promotion or new job. If a hat is bright or large, it usually reflects your desire to attract, show off or be seen. If it is small or demure, it indicates that you want to blend in with other people.

Gloves in a dream suggest that you feel vulnerable and are attempting to protect yourself.

Precious **jewellery** in a dream often signifies good fortune and prosperity. Tarnished jewellery generally signifies fears or uncertainties about money. An image of a **ring** is a symbol of union, of success in relationships or work, or an indication of the changes that surround you.

Earrings are usually a symbol of keenness to hear and understand.

Everyday objects

Books

Books often appear in dreams when you are learning and developing or when you feel there are issues that you want to understand or should understand.

Camera

To be photographed in a dream usually indicates a feeling that you are on show. To photograph others usually reflects your conscious efforts to remember information and difficulties you may be having absorbing information, or it could be a sign that, emotionally, you are hanging on to the present and not going forward into the future.

Cigarettes

Smoking a cigarette in a dream is usually connected to anxiety, perhaps because you have decided to give up smoking but are having problems doing so.

Clocks

Dream clocks usually reflect your fears about time, that there are not enough hours in the day, a feeling that you are always rushing or a worry that you might be unpunctual.

Coins

Losing a copper coin in a dream usually indicates lack of confidence; finding one, increased self-esteem.

If you find a small silver coin in a dream, you might be about to receive money through good luck.

A dream of a large silver coin is often a symbol for inspiration as well as the need to instigate changes in your life.

Furniture

A dream image of antiques is usually a sign of not being up to date with current information or feeling out of sync with your inner self or the rest of the world.

Heirlooms

These are often dream symbols of your expectations or desires, items you wish to purchase, of goods and chattels of great significance or value to you.

Hooks

If you dream of hooks, you may fear being placed in a position where you will be forced to act in a way contrary to your feelings, and you are concerned with how your peer group will judge you.

Jars

Empty jars in a dream generally represent acquisition of a specific skill; full jars, the achievement of competency or proficiency.

Junk

Dreams about junk commonly indicate neglect of important matters which should be addressed without delay. Such a dream might occur when you need to act positively to counter the negative effects of lack of enthusiasm.

Kite

When kites fly high in your dreams they usually represent happiness and achievement.

Knives

A thrown knife in a dream typically represents your fear of gossip or not fitting in with a group.

Ladder

Experiencing difficulty in climbing a ladder commonly indicates that you are exceeding your natural limitations; climbing easily indicates achievement and personal direction.

Letters

To dream of receiving letters announces that prosperous change might be imminent. A dream of outgoing mail might indicate a concern with bills you have to pay.

Letterbox

An empty letterbox in a dream usually indicates that you are waiting for something or waiting to hear from someone. An overflowing letterbox or one drenched by rain often represents your fear that you won't hear from a loved one. You will usually receive money after a dream of a red letterbox. A white letterbox might reflect a feeling of being lost and often is a sign that the subconscious is putting you in touch with memories and fears and helping you to clear them out.

Mirrors

To dream about a mirror traditionally signifies acceptance of oneself and others.

The image of a broken mirror usually occurs in a dream when your beliefs are being questioned by others or you are comparing their beliefs with your own. It might also indicate the shattering of an illusion in your life.

Reflections of yourself in a dream mirror might mean you are trying, unsuccessfully, to come to terms with unhappy feelings, perhaps those of grief or loss.

Seeing other people in a mirror might reflect the dreamer's wistful, hopeful, or perhaps melancholy state of mind.

Needles

Whether a sewing needle or a pine needle, a sharply pointed needle typically represents pain or the fear of pain.

Pearls

These are dream images of teardrops, usually indicating that the dreamer is going through a grieving process or fears being emotional.

Scissors

A pair of scissors suggests that something is catching up with you or you are finding it difficult to keep pace with a trying situation.

Shadows

Your own shadow in a dream indicates a sense of acute vulnerability, dislike of your body or fear of lack of acceptance by others.

Another's shadow may mean you are out of touch with what you want in life and unable to see what is being presented to you by others.

Spectacles

Wearing spectacles in a dream suggests an inability to see something properly in your waking life.

If you usually wear spectacles, the dream suggests concern about your eyes.

Telephone

A telephone in a dream suggests that you are waiting for information, or it may be a sign that you are about to experience a dream involving past-life recall.

Umbrella

This image is a signal from the subconscious that you should prepare for change or for extra or heavy work and also indicates emotional release.

Zipper

A dream of an open zipper, especially if it is stuck, usually reflects a sense of exposure when you are not quite finished a project or task.

A closed zipper often indicates that you are ready to perform in a work situation.

A too short zipper may mean you do not have enough material for a project, while a zipper that is too long could be a sign that you have overestimated a situation.

Plants

GARDENS ARE SYMBOLS of growth. In dreams, they represent self-identity and confidence. A flourishing garden commonly indicates this is a period of good fortune in your life and that you are experiencing inner calm and happiness. Blossoms typically represent creativity, that you are very happy with life and looking forward to each day.

If part of the garden is dying, you may be feeling upset, depressed or confused. A dream of plants with drooping leaves suggests your propensity to mood swings and uncertainty.

Trees are widely accepted symbols of determination and strength. They often represent the changes over one's lifetime from childhood through adolescence to adulthood and the ability to see situations from different perspectives.

Bare trees usually mean that there is hard work ahead, and you can't see the reasons for it or the results.

Burnt or scarred trees might mean that you are feeling vulnerable or powerless.

Brightly coloured trees typically signify creativity or change.

Deep, richly coloured trees usually signify spiritual awakening or self discovery.

A palm tree in a dream foretells material gain or a change in attitude that will enable growth.

Herbs generally represent the subtleties of the personality, your innermost emotions.

Nuts tend to feature in the dreams of those saving money for a particular goal. Or they might be a sign that your subconscious is filing away information.

A **four-leaf clover** traditionally represents awareness and prosperity.

Moss is often a symbol of creative or physical fertility.

Food

Preparing food is a common dream symbol of creativity and purpose in life.

A dream of **unfamiliar food** suggests that you feel uncomfortable with your colleagues and acquaintances.

Eating with pleasure might mean acceptance of your physical appearance.

To dream of huge quantities of food or that your appetite is insatiable suggests that you worry about your weight and possible weight gain.

If you dream of delicious food, you are possibly anticipating a pleasant event. If you are eating the most decadent dessert in your dream, you might be feeling the need to act spontaneously and to enjoy something out of the ordinary.

Confectionery commonly represents a self-reward or treat. However, striped candy might indicate some physical disorder.

Icecream usually represents success and acknowledgment that you have done well.

Cow's **milk** traditionally signifies motherhood and the abundance of life. Milk in a jug often represents self-made wealth and success, self-sufficiency and satisfaction.

Eggs usually represent new people coming into your life. Fried eggs might represent fitting into a situation or understanding a situation for what it really is. Broken eggs usually represent vulnerability and uncertainty in personal relationships.

Green **fruit** in a dream usually signifies that you know the outcome of a situation and are preparing for the final stages. Unusual fruit generally represents doubt or confusion, something not feeling quite right in your life.

Animals

IMAGES OF ANIMALS occur in dreams because they are symbols of "natural" feelings, emotions we may be trying to repress. Different species of animals are renowned for specific characteristics. The elephant, for example, is known to be methodical and possesses an impressive memory.

If you dream of an **angry animal**, it is likely that you repress your own anger. If you dream of a **carefree animal**, you might be suppressing a healthy yearning for more freedom and time to explore opportunities for personal growth. **Non-aggressive animals** in dreams generally signify your feelings of trust, contentment and harmony. **Playful animals** typically signify feelings of joyful exuberance.

If you dream of an animal (usually a cat) sitting on top of, or next to, an object that is familiar to you, then it is often the object, not the animal, to which you should pay attention.

If you have seen the same animal in several dreams over months or perhaps years, it might be your animal **totem or guide**. If so, it might appear in your dreams to assist your subconscious in leading you to correct conclusions or decisions. You might find that once you are aware of your animal totem, it will frequently manifest itself in your wakened state in its physical form and also in the form of other images, maybe as a photograph or ornament. If you see an animal in a dream state, watch for any out-of-character actions in the same type of live animal which might indicate that this is your totem animal, coming to you with a message.

Many people turn for guidance to their totem animals in the area of the animal's specially developed ability. For instance, you might request a crow totem for advice on location when you need a more suitable home. If a bear is your totem, you might draw upon it as a source of strength. A deer totem might help you when you urgently need to find safety and security. To dream of an owl totem following an important decision might confirm the wisdom of that decision.

Birds

Flying represents freedom. So when you dream of flying birds or animals, including humans, you may have broken free of restriction, self-imposed or otherwise. You are now free to explore, to move in any direction you choose. Such dreams are common when you are formulating new ideas or investigating your own potential.

Birds themselves have always been powerfully spiritual symbols. If they feature in your dreams, there may be a need to reflect on the direction you are currently taking in life.

Some birds in particular embody a widely acknowledged meaning. The owl represents wisdom. The eagle represents silent strength and clear sight. The crow represents sense of direction — nomadic tribes often followed the path of the crow when looking for food, water or wintering grounds.

Images of birds might also be prophetic. They might indicate that something very powerful is coming into your life or that issues currently concerning you are about to be resolved.

Dream images of birds might also convey a warning to the dreamer. A dream of an owl flying across your path, for example, might mean you should slow down and be more cautious as there could be something dangerous ahead.

A dream of a bird with eggs signifies wealth and gain. A dream of a bird without eggs indicates a fear of loss, the loss of a relationship, or a loss of your sense of self.

Cackling chickens or quacking ducks often represent unwelcome information, repetition, or extreme frustration at not being able to make yourself heard.

Cats

Domestic cats in a dream are generally warnings to put aside self-pity and counter adversity in your life.

Cats moving around you might indicate an awakening of your spiritual growth and sensitivity.

A fighting cat suggests that the dreamer is experiencing internal conflict.

Black cats generally signify superstition and uncertainty and often appear when you are having difficulty determining the difference between fantasy and reality.

Dogs

Dogs usually signify loyalty, protection and unconditional love.

In dreams they can indicate that the dreamer is feeling lonely, unloved and not accepted for themselves. These animals often appear when you have argued or have little contact with a loved one or when you want to share time with other people.

If you dream of a dog in difficulty, it means your own comfort level is under threat from the people or events in your life.

Barking, playful dogs indicate that your own mood is companionable and fun-seeking or that you will soon enjoy an exciting event or special occasion in which you are the focus of attention.

Elephants

These fascinating animals might frequent your dreams when you are concerned about remembering something important — during times of study, for example.

Because they are large, slow-moving animals, elephants might also signify your concern about excess weight or a project that isn't moving as fast as you would like. However, the hippopotamus is a more common dream symbol for weight problems.

Horses

The speed and grace of the galloping horse in a dream can indicate eagerness for change, anticipating a new venture in life. Or it may be a sign that you are entering a very happy period in your life.

A white horse in a dream usually signifies fertility and the presence of prosperity and success. This dream often appears during pregnancy as a woman prepares for the birth.

Insects

In dreams, insects can represent petty issues which cause enormous irritation.

Large, flying insects indicate that someone in your life has a problematic attitude which you can't seem to make clear to them.

Large, slow-moving, slug-like insects suggest that you have overeaten or otherwise over-indulged.

Swarms of bees or ants might represent a fear of detail.

Dreams of small insects might represent your fastidiousness.

To dream of ants, particularly those building nests or hunting for food, might also signify deep-seated anxiety or perfectionism. Or perhaps something will not be as you expect it.

Vibrantly coloured moths and butterflies in your dreams traditionally represent prosperity and success.

If their colouring is dark or lacking in distinction, your achievements might pass without recognition.

Dreams of these insects might also indicate a loss of money or fear of a shortage of money.

A white moth may be a warning to watch your spending.

An iridescent moth usually represents lost or elusive opportunities, particularly for making money.

Lion

A dream of a powerful creature like a lion or tiger generally signifies your inner strength whether you're on the attack or on the defensive.

Experiencing fear of these animals in a dream suggests that you fear what you see in yourself.

A roaring lion indicates that you are taking a stand in life.

A very still lion implies that you are prepared to respond to a new challenge.

Marine creatures

Fish can be seen as a sign of the times, the Age of Aquarius. In dreams, they usually signify the awakening of your intuition and inspiration, the emergence of great ideas, your enthusiasm and excitement about coming news and events.

They might also signify future movement and change of direction in a situation that is currently beyond your control.

The dream image of a shark might occur when you fear that others disregard you or that you are incompetent.

The whale is often a dream symbol of superior creativity, the freedom it demands and the freedom it brings.

Dolphins appear graceful and free, the sounds they make are like laughter. These animals are synonymous with the intellect, happiness and freedom of expression. They are renowned for their potential to communicate with humans. To dream of a dolphin might signify a period of fruitfulness in your life or a reinforcement of spiritual communication or direction.

Mice and rats

Dreaming of mice suggests that you are part of an efficient team or a close-knit family or group. It indicates an individual is fitting into a group situation, be it family, work or school.

Rats suggest that you are feeling suspicious or that you are an outsider, an observer rather than a participant.

It is unusual to dream of rodents unless you are involved in certain matters, probably financial, in which you doubt the integrity of other parties.

Monkeys

Monkey dreams typically reflect the mischievous, playful side of your nature.

Rabbits

A rabbit in a dream may herald the arrival of a new baby.

Reptiles

Snakes, lizards and other small, venomous animals commonly represent uncertainty and deceit. They usually occur in dreams at times when you suspect someone is not to be trusted, that you are being secretly persecuted, unfairly judged, misunderstood or excluded.

They might also occur when you are not adequately voicing your opinion.

Reptiles might represent conflict with an overbearing person or someone whose actions are unacceptable to you, or perhaps you are unable or unwilling to behave as they desire.

However, a dream image of an alligator traditionally signifies the jaws of justice and is usually a symbolic reminder of some wrongdoing that you cannot admit to yourself or others.

Sheep

If you dream of sheep you might be pleased by acceptance into a group or by the development of a new skill to a standard equal to that of people around you.

The image of a shepherd traditionally relates to spiritual protection.

Spiders

Large, dark spiders in dreams usually signify a change for the better, a reward after a period of famine (particularly financial). The bigger the spider, the better for you.

Other colours generally signify that you do not accurately understand the value or purpose of an offer to you.

A purple or lavender hue around a spider indicates a spiritual gift, possibly from your spirit guide.

A redbacked spider suggests that there will be a price to pay for something you desire.

A yellow-striped spider indicates that you will receive a reward for your work.

Dead spiders suggest fear or uncertainty. As soon as possible after you dream of destroying a spider, consciously affirm that you wish to release any fear of the spider and to accept its particular gift to you.

Images of concealed spiders might signify your fear of the future.

When spiders are swinging from a web in your dreams, it is possible that good fortune will enter your life.

Spiders resting in a web suggest a need for comfortable accommodation.

If a spider is entangled in a web, you may be uncomfortable in your sleeping place or stifled in your daily life.

Cobwebs alone are usually symbols of wealth and prosperity, of a change for the better in circumstance.

Unicorns

The appearance of a unicorn, the symbol of purity and truth, in a dream represents a break from reality and the need to be less serious about life. It could be time to let your inner child out to play.

Unicorns can also be a powerful suggestion from deep within your subconscious to let you know that you are in charge and nothing can go wrong. At such a time, you may feel very successful and notice that other people are aware of your achievements.

The natural world

YOUR HIDDEN FEELINGS are exposed in the climate of your dreams. If you dream of **fair weather**, you are probably feeling happy with life.

Bright, sunny dreams usually express your creative expansion and potential. They suggest that, in regard to the subject you are dreaming about, you are in control and feeling comfortable and settled.

Dreaming of a fair sky often means that opportunities are open to do whatever you want to do.

Dark, gloomy weather in your dreams represents your fears and reservations, and the realm of the unknown. It may mean that you are unable to pinpoint exactly what is disturbing you about a person or situation.

To dream of **cyclones, tornados or hurricanes** may be a sign that things are bigger than you imagined and you have a fear of being out of control.

Dreaming of an **earthquake** might mean that your sleep is being disturbed by outside noises.

Floods or tidal waves in dreams typically represent the release of emotion and tension.

A dream image of the **moon** frequently signals that you will enjoy a flash of inspiration or creativity, experience success, the pleasure of increased wealth, perhaps an inheritance. For a woman, it may be a signal of ovulation.

Stars shining brightly are usually symbols of the early flickering of new ideas. Dim and minuscule stars might indicate some difficulty with eyesight or headaches.

Images such as **monumental landforms, prehistoric animals, impenetrable jungles or vast deserts** often suggest feelings of inadequacy and a belief that you are fated to fail.

Water is the most powerful of the physical elements: earth, fire, air and water. Water automatically takes the shape of any vessel it is placed in, it flows easily around obstacles, and in time will cut through solid stone. This is one of the most powerful signs in your dream imagery. When you dream that you are in a pleasant, watery environment you are probably being nurtured by life, feeling balanced and satisfied with your progress, confident of reaching your potential. Calm and inviting water suggests the development of your imagination or a new stage in your life.

A dream of rough, turbulent water suggests that you are processing change, dealing with associated uncertainties.

Icy cold water might be a sign that you are feeling out of your depth.

If the water is moving slowly towards unknown land, it generally suggests an acceptance of new information. If it's moving quickly, it usually represents a change that you can't keep up with.

An image of water flowing over rocks or of a tributary flowing into a mainstream indicates that you are approaching a more tranquil stage.

Fast-flowing rivers or waterfalls usually represent cleansing and renewal, the total release of a dysfunctional part of your life.

Placid streams and rivers indicate inner calm.

If you dream that you are being washed away by a mass of water, it suggests you are unable to control how you feel.

Being caught in a current suggests that you are concerned that you don't have an opinion of your own so you just agree with others.

A dream in which you cannot swim to land is symbolic of a fear of failure.

A dream of drowning might be a warning from the subconscious that you have more work than you can handle and so are falling behind and cannot catch up. Or it may represent debts you fear you cannot pay.

If you are able to breathe underwater in a dream, it suggests that you have discovered that you are more capable than you thought or that things have worked out easier than you imagined they would.

Rain that is soft and gentle in a dream is clearing to the mind, opening it to new thinking. Heavy rain might mean that you are overloaded with too much pressure or too much to think about and you are not feeling as well as possible.

A dream of **mud** suggests you are feeling you are stuck in a situation.

Crystalline **snow and ice** are classic symbols of purity and clarity, inspiration, spirituality and transformation — the cleansing of the body and the mind.

A dream of heavy snow or ice often represents fear or apprehension.

Feeling **hot** or stifled in a dream suggests that your immediate surroundings are too warm for your physical comfort during sleep. Rarely, if ever, does heat in a dream have other symbolic messages unless it also includes smoke or fire.

Smoke generally indicates feelings of frustration and difficulty in expressing them.

Flames, like ice, can be a symbol of ritual cleansing.

However, fire around you can also suggest that you are trying to find a solution to an out-of-control situation.

If the fire is emanating from you, it could suggest that you are going to be very successful at an activity you are about to try.

Seeing a familiar person alive and well but surrounded by fire could also be a sign of great success and prosperity.

A dream in which you see a stranger in the background and fire in the foreground might reflect the efforts of a dead friend or relative to communicate with you.

A burning building often indicates helplessness and fear — perhaps you believe you have gone too far or said too much and are unable to repair some damage that you have done to a relationship or situation.

Buildings

IT IS OFTEN SAID that the space a person lives in represents themselves. The more knowledge you have about a building in your dream, the more knowledge you are likely to have of yourself.

If you are looking at a building's **exterior** in your dream and don't know what you will find inside, it suggests that you are in the process of uncovering something within yourself or in someone else but have yet to go far beyond the surface.

An **empty house or a strange environment** might signify a soul-searching period of your life, or a change in your awareness that you are finding difficult to deal with.

To dream of **constructing** a building is often a sign that you are self-directed in your waking life.

If the building is a **castle**, your dream indicates that you are probably developing your individuality.

If it is more like a **fortress**, you might need protection from yourself as well as from other sources.

A **maze-like building** could indicate that you are caught in a confusing web of circumstances and you don't know the way out.

A dream about a **small** building might signify doubts about your present accommodation, perhaps you are being forced to leave and don't know where you will go. Or it might indicate career uncertainties.

A **large** building suggests that the dreamer is excited about the future, ready for new activities or more work.

If the building is **tall**, you might desire to be distinctive or it might be a subconscious suggestion that your potential is only just being tapped into.

If the building is a **home**, it is usually a symbol of security and stability.

If the house is **bright and cheery**, you are likely to be feeling good about yourself.

A dream image of a **very clean** house usually reflects being on top of life and ready for more challenges.

A **dusty** house usually indicates that you are overdue for a rest.

Dreams of **damp and dank** houses sometimes come to us when we are recovering from illness.

A **derelict** house might be a subconscious expression of feeling left out or that no one cares about you.

When you dream of an **overcrowded** house, chances are that you feel that someone or something is cramping your style, or perhaps people are encroaching on your living space or your partner is taking up too much of the bed.

A house **filled with papers or books** suggests that you are overloaded with work and unable to cope with the demands being placed on you.

Dreams about **large and airy** rooms are often symbols of your acceptance that you still have more to learn.

Small, cramped rooms often feature in the dreams of overloaded people who would like to get out and enjoy themselves but have too many obligations stopping them.

To dream of yourself in a **basement or cellar** is usually an expression of your fear that others will discover your secrets. If looking down into a basement, you might feel that things are going on around you that you don't understand or that you are being excluded by others.

Dreams of **toilets** usually represent feelings of extreme vulnerability.

Halls and corridors in a dream might indicate getting in touch with deep seated fears, uncertainties, or problems.

Walls signify obstacles and restrictions.

Open **doorways** typically invite the conscious mind to explore opportunities being offered in life.

Passing through a doorway in a dream typically represents embarking upon a new and exciting period in your life and might herald new developments in your career, relationships, or home.

Running through a doorway and banging a door behind might be a sign that you are weighing your positive attitude against your uncertainties to determine what the outcome of a situation may be.

Being chased through doors might indicate the need to escape from someone in your waking life. Locking the door behind you suggests that this situation is over-whelming and you are unable to deal with it at the moment.

A dream of a closed door is often an expression of indecision or despair, or you may be concerned about whether opportunities will present themselves.

If a closed door is bolted, you might be feeling locked into the life you have created and blocked from being able to change it.

A door lock without a key suggests that you find it difficult to express emotions or you desire privacy.

If the building in your dream has lots of **windows** or large windows, it usually indicates that you are happy with life, open and communicative with people, and everything seems to be going right for you at present.

A dream in which you exit through the window suggests a release of restrictions, running away from problems.

Curtains blowing in the wind are frequently symbols of inner harmony and higher spiritual learning.

Dreams of rooms crowded with **furniture** usually signify your need to lighten your domestic load or to simplify or tidy your accommodation.

A dream of a sparsely furnished environment might occur when you are unsupported, lacking comfort and feeling sorry for yourself.

Stairs leading nowhere suggest that you are feeling at a loss as to where life is taking you, that you are not getting what you want, or that a relationship is not progressing.

Walking upstairs or going up in an elevator is usually a sign of travel. Going down usually means you have been disappointed.

A dream of a **rooftop** suggests the release of restrictions and blocks. You may feel you are being evaluated in your waking life if you dream you are watched from a rooftop.

A **gate** swinging back and forth in a dream generally indicates something going out of your life and something coming in. A locked and chained gate suggests you are being stubborn and not allowing something to come into your life. A wide open gate often indicates acceptance of what is on offer to you.

Situations & surroundings

IF YOU DREAM of a **hole** in the ground you might be entering a situation in your waking life with the expectation that you will lose control of its direction.

A **maze** is a dream image that reflects the subconscious searching for answers, trying to understand the changes that are occurring in your life. You might find the end of the maze in your dream when your conscious mind has found the answers to your questions. Mazes show you that you need to stop running around in circles and determine what you want out of life.

A **park**, on the other hand, usually reflects balance in the family, at home, with yourself and the people around you.

If you dream you are back at **school**, in your wakened state you might be feeling that you have much to learn. A dream of a teacher might be a sign of inner imbalance, perhaps a health problem. An image of yourself as a teacher might indicate that you have grown and want to share your knowledge with others.

To dream of a **playground** is often a sign that you are considering your future. A dream of an empty, slowly rocking swing might suggest contemplating different points of view. Playing on the swing represents being able to understand these varied perspectives.

Dream images of **shopping malls** generally signify the entire process involved in the dreamer's transition from a smaller to a larger group. This type of image might occur when you have many new things confronting you at once and you are unable to deal with them all. A very dark shopping mall might represent a big change in your life that you are uncertain about. A dream that you are alone or with strangers in a shopping mall suggests a move to a new environment.

An image of yourself at **work** in a pleasant environment with friendly colleagues suggests that you are happy with your workplace and the people there. If the environment is gloomy, it suggests you have problems at work. If your co-workers are argumentative or you are the only worker present, others being strangely absent from your dream, you might be in conflict with your colleagues or worried about losing your job. If others are able to enter the workplace but you cannot, you might be planning to give notice but don't know how to express your intentions.

Dreaming that you have an enormous amount of work to do might be a warning that you are using work as an excuse not to look at other issues in your life.

A dream that you are contentedly immersed in work might be an expression of your creativity in reality or your subconscious showing you the solution to a problem that you have not been able to solve in your waking state.

Parties and celebrations in dreams reflect the joy of success and relaxation. You might be feeling relief at the passing of a time or event that you were unsure of or feared. If you see yourself at a dinner party, it might reflect a need to be more sociable in your waking life.

Transport & travel

TRANSPORT AND TRAVEL in dreams generally reflect imminent change and movement in your life and your attitude towards it.

A dream of an **unknown destination** often indicates that you are unsure of the outcome.

A dream about an **adventure** is difficult to interpret. You need to consider the context of your daily life, the dream's timeframe, setting and cast of characters. Such a dream might be a re-run of a past-life experience or simply the expression of a fantasy.

To dream of **leisurely travel** is a symbol for being very much in control of your life and its direction.

If you see yourself **moving through a scenic landscape**, it could reflect a need to be on your own so you can achieve growth in your ideas and awareness. Such a dream might occur when your life seems overcrowded.

A dream that you are **walking** suggests you are about to have a breakthrough in understanding. This might relate to study or the digestion of information.

Wandering, however, usually indicates that in your wakened state you feel exhausted and frustrated.

Aircraft travel usually suggests you are looking forward to a trip. But, as it involves both flying and movement, it often represents personal growth, creative and intellectual expansion, and new awareness through a fresh stimulus.

Images of an aircraft taking off might signify a launch into a new area whereas an aircraft landing can signal the conclusion of a job or relationship. An aircraft that makes a smooth landing might reflect your conscious awareness that an aspect of your life is coming to an end and you feel that everything will work out. If, however, it is a crash-landing, you are not comfortable with this knowledge. A dream of an aircrash usually means that you feel out of control and unsure of what to do. If you dream that you experience great turbulence while in the air, it might warn of uncertainties ahead of you.

Sea travel also tends to represent excitement about the future.

When you dream that you are standing on a dock, watching a boat depart, it is possible that you are missing out on an activity in which you want to be involved. A boating accident might represent a cancellation of some scheduled event.

Catching a **train** generally indicates that you are on schedule for something that you want or are going to be involved in but if you miss the train (or any other form of transport) you have probably left it too late.

Being in a **car** with others suggests that you are developing friendships and alliances and a broader understanding of life in the process.

If the trip is frustrating, perhaps you feel out of control in your waking life. If the car is like a jeep, navigating bumpy roads, it suggests you are surmounting obstacles in your waking life.

As either the driver or passenger in a car going to a meeting with others, you might be about to make new friends and acquaintances.

A car crash usually represents a conflict or argument with a friend or friends.

A **bridge** is a common symbol of transition or growth. If you find you are on one side of a bridge, then you might be preparing yourself for changes that you feel uncertain about. If you are in the middle of the bridge then you are probably growing as a person and about to enter a new period in your life. If you have reached the far side of a bridge, you might have conquered a fear or resolved an issue which you had reservations about.

If a short, blocked **tunnel** appears in your dream, it suggests that currently you are unable to grasp a concept but are approaching a solution to the problem. A dark and endless tunnel might be a sign that you never seem to find what you are looking for.

The arts

SEEING YOURSELF **on stage** performing might mean that you are not being yourself in your waking life. Perhaps you are projecting an image of what you believe others expect and you are being judged on that false image. If there is no one in the audience in your dream then you might be letting yourself know that you are unhappy with the situation.

To dream of **acting** is a possible sign that you are unable to express your emotions directly to someone.

Dancing in a dream suggests happiness, excitement and enthusiasm, stability and an internal balance. If it is ballet, it is likely that you are entering a period of self-approval where you are starting to accept the creative side of your personality or that of someone close to you.

A dream in which you or another **draw, paint or sculpt** might be regarded as a subconscious expression of your creativity.

The act of **writing** or images of words generally reflects a desire to understand and to be clearly understood.

An image of ornate or old-worldly lettering often indicates the reactivation of your creativity, your sense of beauty or your appreciation of nature which once flowed through your life but which you have since suppressed. It might be a sign to free your mind from the daily grind.

The sound of **music** might accompany the recall of a past life in which you performed or appreciated music. Music might also express the message of the dream if it provides the main focus. Pay attention to the lyrics if the words are clear. Soft, gentle music is usually a symbol of peace, comfort and tranquillity. Loud, boisterous music might indicate that you have been nagged to do something and you wish to escape that pressure, or you may have been procrastinating. Composers and songwriters often receive melodies or lyrics in their dreams as their subconscious works in conjunction with their conscious desire to create music.

Figures of fantasy

DREAM **monsters or hooded figures** conventionally represent the fear of the unknown, fear of the future.

Dreams of **aliens** usually indicate that you are aware that there are matters beyond your comprehension, or that you fail to understand others' views of you.

Elves and fairies are frequently signs that your inner child is active, exploring and developing. They are usually harbingers of happiness and success. When your subconscious delivers a dream with a fairytale subject or conclusion, it is probably encouraging you to do your utmost to ensure positive outcomes in your endeavours.

Seeing yourself as **royalty** is usually a symbol of your confidence and self-assurance. Seeing others as monarchs often indicates that you gauge them as superior to yourself, embodying qualities that you admire and wish you shared. Such dreams can also signify respect for your parents.

Published by Lansdowne Publishing Pty Ltd
Sydney, Australia

Designer: Kathie Baxter Smith
Illustrator: Penny Lovelock

First published in 1995
Reprinted 1997, 1998

Formatted in 12 pt M Perpetua on Quark Xpress
Printed in Singapore by Tien Wah Press (Pte) Ltd

National Library of Australia Cataloguing-in-Publication Data
Garfield, Frank
Dreams : unlock the secrets to your subconscious.

Includes index.
ISBN 1 86302 410 7.

1. Dreams. 2. Dream interpretation. I. Stewart-Garfield, Rhondda. II. Title.
154.63